A souvenir guide

Little Moreton Hall

Cheshire

M000267750

❧ National Trust

Welcome to the Tudor Manor House

Little Moreton Hall is a Tudor house that defies expectations.

One of the best-known half-timbered buildings in Britain, Little Moreton Hall rises from the flat Cheshire plains that surround it, its riotously decorative timbers as impressive now as when they were first hewn, carved and hefted into place some 500 years ago.

This was a house that was built to impress. It is a lasting reminder of the sophistication and craftsmanship of the Tudor era – a building of such structural ingenuity, dazzling carpentry, plasterwork, painting and glazing, that to this day it is the envy of many who visit.

Defying gravity

Yet this is also a house that buckles beneath its own weight. The massive burden of its stone-slabbed roof bears down on crooked, sagging timbers, apparently threatening to send the lot tumbling into the moat below. So the question many ask when they first arrive is not how Little Moreton Hall came to be built – but how it still stands at all.

To answer that question, we must first understand who built Little Moreton Hall – and who saved it. For almost all of its history it was owned by one family, the Moretons, and the story of the house is essentially also their story. Never sold, it was passed down through successive generations and then let out to tenant farmers for over 200 years before finally being vested in the National Trust in 1938.

'[I] shall not forget the thrill as I topped the rise after Scholar Green, walking from Kidsgrove Station, and saw the front of the old black and white house in spring sunshine confronting me. It has been in my heart and dreams ever since.'

Bishop Abraham, writing in his notebook about his first visit to the house he would go on to inherit and, later, pass on to the National Trust

Left The north range, looking onto the courtyard

Right A view across the moat to the end of the garderobe and south range windows

Who Were the Moretons?

If we know one thing about the Moretons, it is that they could afford to be ostentatious.

Powerful local landlords from the 13th century, the Moretons probably increased their wealth following disasters both natural and manmade: by buying up land thrown onto the market after the Black Death of 1348 and during the Dissolution of the Monasteries (1536–41).

It was an acquisition policy that paid off. By the mid-16th century, the Moretons were in control of some 550 hectares (1,360 acres) of land. It was mainly the income from this estate that allowed them to build Little Moreton Hall more or less continuously for over 100 years, expanding and improving it from the early 16th century up until the Civil War in 1642. By then, the house as we know it was intact, but its development was called to an abrupt halt. The Moretons backed the Royalists during the war

and their loyalty to the crown – under a punitive Parliamentarian government – marked the start of the Hall's slow, 250-year decline. Yet, as we shall see, the war didn't quite spell the end of the Moretons' dealings with a home that can befuddle as much as it bedazzles.

A Tudor puzzle

You might assume that because Little Moreton Hall has only ever been owned by one family, it would be rich in records and archives. In fact, the opposite is true. The Moretons may have built a noble-looking house, but they were not a noble family, and their primary political dalliance – during the Civil War – ended in disaster. As such, there are few records that tell us about their lives, save for inventories taken on the death of various heads of the household, legal documents and a modest number of personal journals and letters.

Little remains of what was once inside the house, too. In fact, only three original items, listed in the inventories taken in 1563 and 1599, are definitely still in situ: the 'cupborde of boxes' and 'great rounde table' in the Great Parlour, and the table found in the Great Hall. The inventory also mentions pewter tableware, though the pieces in this room now are more likely to be from around the 18th century.

Since the Hall was bequeathed to the Trust in 1938, an enormous amount of research has been carried out in an attempt to shed light on Little Moreton's shadowy corners. In 2012, a full architectural survey provided drawings of

Above The pewter pieces in situ in 1929

the house so detailed – right down to the size and position of each peg hole – that we could, if we ever needed to, rebuild it exactly as it is today.

Yet this survey also raised more questions than it answered. So the information contained within this book comes with a caveat: there are some things that we may never know for sure about Little Moreton Hall. We can only make an educated guess as to when certain parts of the building were constructed. Little Moreton Hall is a fascinating, 500-year-old puzzle – and a place that sometimes guards its past as fiercely as the wolf on the Moreton's family crest.

Left The 'great rounde table', mentioned in the 16th-century inventories, can be found in the Great Parlour

Above The Moretons' family crest, featuring the fearsome wolf

Tudor Life

The Tudor era (1485–1603) was one of great social, political and religious upheaval.

This was a result of a number of events, from royal divorce and the creation of the Church of England under Henry VIII, to the population and economic growth experienced during Elizabeth I's long reign.

Although society was still as hierarchical as it had ever been, social mobility became more common in this period and hard-working men of a non-noble birth, such as the Moretons, began to climb through the ranks.

Tudor one-upmanship

As a result of this increased social mobility, status symbols took on the utmost importance. Although there had been strict laws around what people were permitted to wear since the 1300s, helping make class distinctions clear, the socially ambitious might claim a higher rank by buying a coat of arms.

And what better way to declare your elevated social standing than with the

Above The grand exterior of Little Moreton Hall, with its expensive glass and chimney stacks, helped to set it apart from the average Tudor house

'No knight under the estate of a lord, esquire or gentleman, nor any other person, shall wear any shoes or boots having spikes or points which exceed the length of two inches under the forfeiture of forty pence.'

One of the series of 14th-century English Sumptuary Laws, dating 1336

construction of such a flamboyant house as Little Moreton Hall? Studded with hard-to-source glass and topped by towering chimney stacks, brickwork and panels, this manor house was very deliberately a class apart.

The English Reformation

The English Reformation enabled Henry to extricate himself from his marriage to Catherine of Aragon, who had failed to produce a male heir. Before the Reformation divorce was prohibited by the Church, and, in 1527, Henry's request to the Pope that his marriage be annulled was rejected. So from 1532, legislation was passed appointing the King as head of the church.

The move was at least tolerated by most of Henry's subjects, though there were some concerns, for example from citizens worried about the dismantling of the charitable systems constructed by the church or from women fearful of what the King's attitude to divorce meant for them. But the biggest threat to Henry came from monks who remained loyal to the Pope. So Henry's advisors found various reasons to take control of their land in what came to be known as the 'Dissolution of the Monasteries'. This meant a lot of land previously owned by the Catholic church was sold off, allowing families like the Moretons to build up their estates.

Above right Despite the influx of money brought in from the Dissolution of the Monasteries, King Henry VIII (1491–1547) was continually close to financial ruin, partly because of his many continental wars and partly because he was a very extravagant spender

Would you like your own coat of arms?
Individuals and companies can still apply for their own coat of arms even if they're not nobility – if they're willing to pay (though not all requests will be granted). One notable example is the Middleton family, who had one commissioned prior to the now-Duchess of Cambridge's marriage to the Duke of Cambridge in 2011 (see picture, left).

Tudor house-building

The construction of timber-framed buildings was a highly skilled job carried out by leading craftsmen in their field.

Unlike most building methods, which stack blocks one atop the other and rely on gravity to keep them together, these homes were formed of a series of prefabricated frames held together by complex pegged joints.

The timber
Before the frames could be made, the master carpenter would select the trees to be used. Even at this early stage, everything would have been meticulously worked out. Gangs of tree fellers and labourers felled the trees using axes, saws and adzes. Each log was squared up by three men (the log suspended on trestles, one man sawing from above, two men from below) to create what was known as boxed heart timber, strong enough to be used throughout a building. These squared timbers were sawed into shape, or sometimes halved by driving in wedges, to reveal the heart wood, the hardest part usually used for exteriors.

The framing yard

Usually an off-site location, here frames would be laid out in full size using strings, lines and pegs, the uprights first, the roof trusses on top and the cross beams laid over and marked for jointing. Everything would be marked down to the last detail before the mortises and tenons were cut (the most common types of joints) and peg holes drilled.

Known as carpenters' marks, marks at the corners of joints allowed pieces to be cut out flat and then reassembled in 3D, at height – almost like a flat-pack house. Some of these marks are still clearly visible at Little Moreton Hall, such as on the timbers of the south range (in the courtyard close to the Chapel).

Raising the frames

Large stones were used as the foundations of the house. These were laid while frames were being made; the beams laid on the foundation, and numbered vertical posts fitted into these beams. Most of the assembly work was done using only rope and pulley. Each storey was built one at a time; the ceiling of each level was simply put in place and then became the base for the next level. Similarly, brick fireplaces were built to ceiling height one floor at a time, growing at the same rate as the rest of the house. The staircase provided additional strength, the main vertical newel posts made from single timbers. In the case of the staircase in Little Moreton Hall's south range, the long newel post came from a tree that was around – or possibly over – seven metres high.

Finishing

The smaller panels formed by the frame were filled in with oak laths (small strips of wood) and then lime plastered and whitewashed.

Right above **Detail of a carpenter's mark on two beams outside the South Chamber**

Right below **An example of damaged plasterwork**

Not so black and white

Little Moreton Hall may be known as a black-and-white house, but when built it was actually silver (the colour oak fades to over time) and cream. It was probably the Victorian period when the timbers were tarred, in the mistaken belief that it preserves the wood. Tudor limewash contained impurities which gave it more of a buttermilk cream colour than white. Contemporary repairs to sections of timber are kept in their original, pale state.

The Tudor calendar

Tudor life revolved around the agricultural calendar, with the patterns of planting and harvest at the centre of life. These festivals gave those at Little Moreton Hall a rhythm by which to live and anticipate holidays and feast days.

Easter

Easter Sunday was the most important feast day of the Tudor calendar. It was also one of the old quarter days of the calendar, which marked the changing of the seasons. These became the time when rents and tithes were due, servants were hired, and debts were paid. Following a church service, a family would return home for an extravagant feast including eggs, cheese and

Above John Nash's hand-coloured lithograph depicting Tudor celebrations at Little Moreton Hall, from his four-volume work *Mansions of England in the Olden Times*

meats, all of which were banned during Lent (then a 6.5-week period of fasting, abstinence and praying that ended on Easter Sunday).

May Day
May Day marked the start of the summer – a time of fertility – and a celebration of completing the sowing of that year's crops. Festivities were suitably joyous, with the crowning of a May Queen, Morris dancing and dancing around a (at that time ribbonless) maypole.

Midsummer
Midsummer festivities developed as rites of purification, protection and blessing to ensure a summer of good weather (essential to healthy crops). The celebration coincided with the summer solstice – the main events took place on Midsummer's Eve and continued five days later on the feast of St Peter & St Paul. Elaborate parades took place, houses were decorated with floral garlands and a communal bonfire was the focus for celebrations with plentiful food, drink, music and dancing.

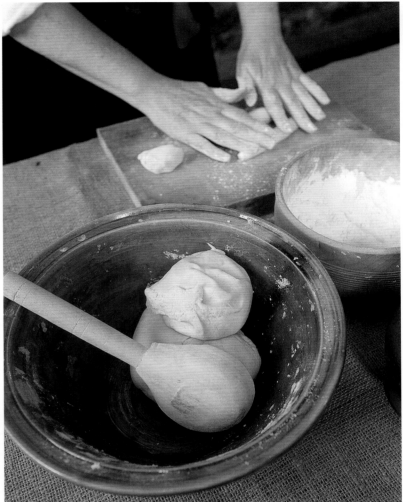

Lammas
Celebrated on the first of August, the first grain harvest, or Lammas (Loaf Mass), marked the end of the Tudor summer. Households brought a loaf of bread made from that first harvest to church.

Above Its name a contraction of 'loaf mass', Lammas was the first harvest festival of the year, and a thanksgiving of grain and bread – the first fruits of the harvest

Left Corn dollies were traditionally cut from the last sheath of corn in the harvest

Michaelmas & goose fairs

The end of the harvest was similarly celebrated. In particular, farmers' debts were due post-harvest; as payment, many presented their landlords with a goose – particularly tasty at this time of year as they fed on left-over grains in the fields post-harvest. Consequently goose fairs have become associated with Michaelmas.

The mop fair

Because servants were hired at Michaelmas, mop fairs sprang up – hiring fairs where hopeful employees advertised their skills via their dress and tokens carried (maids carrying mops, shepherds with a tuft of wool on their hat, and so on). Once hiring was complete, revelries began.

Right A witches' mark, found in the Great Parlour. These were thought to ward off evil spirits – especially important at Hallowtide, as Tudors believed supernatural forces were particularly prevalent at this time

A long tradition

One act of charity undertaken during Hallowtide was the giving of specially baked bread – 'soul cakes' – to the poor in return for prayers for the souls of the departed. It was a custom that continued to the 19th century, with visitors expecting to receive cakes, apples, drink, or money at each house for their singing a souling rhyme. This eventually became 'trick or treating' as we know it today.

Above At hiring – or mop – fairs, craftsmen carried items signifying their trade

Astbury Wakes

Local to Little Moreton Hall, this festival took place on the Sunday between 4 and 10 October. Crowds gathered for a 'dedication of the church', a service followed by a procession and, later, the cockfighting and bear baiting for which Congleton became famous.

Hallowtide

A three-day festival, Hallowtide incorporated All Hallows or Hallowe'en on 31 October, All Saints on 1 November and All Souls the following night. It focused on helping the souls of those in purgatory. Bells were rung and charms used to ward off evil spirits, while people performed acts of charity and prayed for their dearly departed.

'He who eats goose on Michaelmas day/ Shan't money lack or debts pay.'

Tudor rhyme linking eating goose at Michaelmas to good luck for the following year.

Yuletide

Yuletide was the biggest festival in the Tudor calendar, spanning 12 days from 25 December until 6 January. Almost all of those dates were taken up by different saints' days. No one went to work; instead, there were visits to neighbours, mystery plays, and song and dance, alongside the burning of the Yule Log and the making of 'minced pyes' whose 13 ingredients represented Christ and his apostles.

Above A replica Tudor band, Piva, at Christmas

Below The Great Board featuring a replica Tudor Yuletide feast during celebrations at Little Moreton Hall

The Moretons

Agriculture, land and argument make up most of what we know about the earliest Moretons, a family that took its name from the Old English that means 'a farm at a marsh'.

These Moretons appear to have been rather argumentative if records are anything to go by, although the fact that most surviving documents are legal ones may explain why. As for Little Moreton Hall, its construction was primarily down to four successive Moretons – all but one of them called William.

William Moreton I (d.1526)

William Moreton I displayed some of his family's alleged contrariness when, in 1513, he was involved in a dispute with Thomas Rode of nearby Odd Rode over who should sit 'highest' at Astbury Church. It was an argument surprisingly common in Tudor England; the closer to the altar you sat, the more important you were deemed to be. Church squabbles aside, it is William I we have to thank for the oldest surviving parts of Little Moreton Hall:

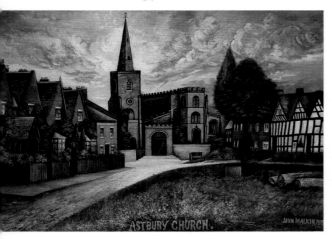

ASTBURY CHURCH.   JOHN MALKIN

he built the east range and the Great Hall in the first decade of the 16th century.

William Moreton I married Alys Brereton (year unknown); the Breretons were an old and noteable local family and their coat of arms can be seen in the stained glass in the Great Hall.

William Moreton II (c.1510–63)

The second William continued his father's work, further extending the house. He built the north-west wing and porch in about 1546, while in 1559 more fashionable work was carried out by the carpenter, Richard Dale, including installing a first floor and the two bay windows that stand in the courtyard. Further improvements, including the construction of the south range, were begun shortly before William's death.

John Moreton (c.1541–98)

The family's financial stability continued, with William's son having enough time and money to continue extending the house until his death. It was John who, in around 1580, decorated the Little Parlour and Chapel, both of whose stunning wall paintings tell us about changing social and religious attitudes in Elizabethan England.

William Moreton III (1574–1654)

Of all of these early Moretons, William III did the least to Little Moreton, adding only the brew and bake houses. He instead concentrated on his large and, as it turned out, expensive family (see pages 16–17). Little Moreton Hall was a welcoming place under William and his wife,

Left Astbury Church, the scene of William Moreton's scuffle with his neighbour, painted by John Malkin in 1918

Above Details of John Moreton's painted panelling in the Little Parlour, which dates from c.1580

What do the wall paintings tell us?

The paintings demonstrate the growth in Protestantism in the country at the time. This is shown through the use of words rather than pictures. Also the Biblical text is in English, rather than priestly Latin; this meant more people would be able to understand the word of God without having a priest translate.

Jane's, stewardship, with cousins, siblings and children all coming to rely on their hospitality. Cousin 'Jack' Booth was so much part of the household that he had his own room, and two of William's siblings lived with their brother. William and Jane had nine surviving children of their own. It was perhaps just as well that Jane had gone through exhaustive negotiations to secure her (considerable) inheritance before she married William – the pair appear to have bankrolled numerous members of their family throughout their married lives.

The Moretons' fall

Although William Moreton III may have provided shelter for his family, he couldn't protect them from the gathering storm – or even from themselves.

His eldest son, John, got thrown out of Christ's College, Cambridge, choosing instead to lead a less-than-learned life in London, largely funded by his father. John's brother (another William) similarly found himself 'more inclined to an other kinde of life' and pursued a career at sea. Both were passed over when it came to their inheritance, with the house left to William's third son, Edward.

But fortune did not favour Edward, who, despite graduating with a Masters degree from Oxford, found himself apparently unemployable. It was a similar story for younger brothers Peter and Philip. They all leaned on their father for support. At one point, a depressed Edward gave up looking for work and returned to Little Moreton Hall. At the same time, William wrote from a Virginia tobacco plantation describing clothes reduced to rags.

But eventually the tide turned. Philip found a place in chambers, Peter became an English Agent in Turin and Edward began a career that would eventually see him become vicar of Sefton in Lancashire. Even John managed to get some sort of job. And then, just as things were improving, the Civil War started.

> 'I now despair of his well-doing here… your young gentleman was got to a bad house by Peterhouse together with another rakestrel.'
>
> John Moreton's college tutor writing to John's father to recommend his son be removed.

Left A letter from John Moreton's college tutor to John's father, seemingly reporting an incidence of blasphemy

Above An eyewitness representation of the execution of King Charles I in 1649

The Moretons' war

The Civil War reached its bloody hand into all corners of England, and Little Moreton Hall could no more escape its reach than Charles I could escape the executioner's axe. As the battle between Royalists and Parliamentarians raged, William Moreton III was arrested. We don't quite know why, but it was probably because they were Monarchists, or had other non-Parliamentarian loyalties.

William was eventually released, but in 1643 his estate was confiscated (as was Edward's), and the pair forced to live at enemy headquarters. William's daughters, Ann and Jane, remained at Little Moreton and rented the estate back from the government, although at high rates and on terms apparently designed to force them into destitution.

By the time William was allowed to return, he found the family's finances in a terrible state. Already stretched before the war, what was left had been shredded by a punitive Parliamentarian government. This was not helped by the huge costs run up by the Parliamentary soldiers, who, along with their horses, were billeted at the Hall for short periods at a time during the Civil War. With fines owed to the state in the region of £641 (the equivalent of about £94,980 today), William set about selling what he could, but when he died he left debts of around £4,000 (worth over £600,000 today). In the space of just one generation, the Moretons had gone from wealthy to near ruined – with huge implications for the future of Little Moreton Hall.

The Moretons' tenants

Edward Moreton suffered alongside his father during the war, and afterwards returned to his home (and his work) in Sefton. The care of the impoverished Hall fell to his siblings Ann, Jane and Philip, though it appears that the death of their father seems to have been some sort of tipping point: never again would a Moreton choose to live permanently at the house they had inherited.

Ann died in 1658, followed by Philip in 1669, and Jane a few years later. With no one living at Little Moreton, and Edward's son, William Moreton IV, off pursuing a clerical career in Ireland, the house was rented out for over 200 years, first to relatives and then to a succession of tenant farmers. Although the family visited – and certainly on occasion kept rooms solely for their use in tenancy agreements – there were few attempts to modernise what by the 18th century had already become an 'old' house.

'Until she became infirm Mrs Dale provided delicious scrambled eggs, home-made scones and tea from a huge pot encased in a woollen cosy resembling a fat brown hen … cows ambled up to the moat (and only occasionally beyond).'

James Lees-Milne, *People and Places*, 1992

The Dales

Consisting of Thomas and Ann Dale and their 14 children, this farming family rented Little Moreton Hall for seven decades, from about 1880 until 1955, first as tenants under the Moretons and then as caretakers for the National Trust. After 1913 the house was open to the public and the Dales gave tours and served teas to the public from 9am until dusk, every day, all year. However, they perhaps didn't appreciate the house's value quite as we do now: for example, the octagonal table in the Great Parlour was used as an ironing board by Kathleen Mary (more commonly known by her middle name) and Winifred Dale during their parents' tenancy.

Even from the beginning of the Dales' time at Little Moreton Hall, the house was clearly deteriorating. In 1887 a Mr Oliver Baker wrote to the Society for the Protection of Ancient Buildings stating that the Hall was 'falling to pieces for want of the most ordinary care. The wall's sinking so as to bulge the panelling as much as two feet.'

Above Ann Dale (seated), surrounded by four of her children (from L-R), Joseph Henry, Jessie, Minnie and Charlie. Records suggest Ann was still farming at the age of 64

Images clockwise from top left

The garden at Little Moreton Hall in 1893

The Great Parlour in 1893, where the Dales served afternoon teas to guests, usually consisting of plates of thinly cut bread and butter with strawberry jam, cake and sometimes scones

Louisa Dale carrying milk. The Dales had 30–35 cows and moving milk from the milking parlour to the dairy was one of the first jobs of the day

Dating from 1893, this photo is probably one of the five Dale daughters (there were 14 siblings in total). We think it is either Maggie or Emily Dale, who would have been 15 and 21 respectively when this was taken

Romantic Decay

In the 18th and 19th centuries, Little Moreton Hall's story became one of neglect, with neither tenants nor landlords giving it the sort of care it so desperately needed.

In 1797, for example, letters between the owner, William Moreton Moreton, and the estate manager mention the Little Parlour's chimney blowing down in a storm. A few years later, and the letters tell of slates and a sheet of lead coming loose from the roof – yet the estate manager happily reports to his master that 'the old Mansion remains the same as

'No gossiping Cicerone has interfered with my wanderings. I had groped and stumbled into every available corner disturbing much ancient dust and alarming many venerable spiders.'

James West, on visiting the house in 1847

Left An oil painting of the exterior of Little Moreton Hall by John Sell Cotman, dated 1807–8

The Black-and-White Revival

Worse was to come. When the artist James West visited Little Moreton in 1847, he found only a few rooms still inhabited: the Victorian rooms to the left of the Great Hall, which were used by the tenant family in residence at the time (either Mary and Frances Thornicroft, or William Rounding). The rest seemed to be being used simply for storage, such as the Chapel, which was functioning as a coal-store, and the garden was overgrown. Yet despite the ignominies of old age, Little Moreton Hall could still impress – or at least influence. It played its part in the Black-and-White Revival, the 19th-century movement led by architects such as T.M. Lockwood and John Douglas who between them turned nearby Chester into the Tudor-style, half-timbered city it is today. For example, Douglas' pupil, Edward Ould, took motifs direct from Little Moreton when designing country houses such as Hill Bark on the Wirral and Wightwick Manor in Staffordshire.

Above A pencil drawing of the Great Hall by John Sell Cotman, 1808. The 'inserted' upper floor had been removed prior to this

Right James West's sketch of the chapel interior, dated 1847

when you saw it last excepting [a] little Plaster being fallen from the end of the Gallery.'

This level of decay lent the building a curious romantic allure; it became the kind of ancient, crumbling pile that appealed to early 19th-century artists such as John Sell Cotman, who drew it for Britton's *Architectural Antiquities of Great Britain* (1808). His sketches depict the grandeur of the Great Hall, yet also show chickens scratching about for food in between the oak furniture, no doubt included by the artist to add to the sense of 'romantic' decay that now surrounded Little Moreton Hall.

Exploring Little Moreton Hall

There are 15 rooms to discover in this 'imperfectly perfect'*, three-storey house. Although mostly empty of furniture, there are many details on the walls, ceilings, floors, windows (and more) to look out for.

* Suzannah Lipscomb,
*A Visitor's Companion to
Tudor England,* 2012

'The close oblique view from the Newcastle-Congleton road of the absurd half-timbered structure, crowned by an unbroken length of gallery window like some fantastic, elongated Chinese lantern, and toppling, if not positively bending over the tranquil water of a moat, the whole an ancient pack of cards about to meet from the first puff of wind its own reflection, is something which once seen can never be forgotten.'

James Lees-Milne, *People and Places*, 1992

The Gatehouse and south range

When visiting Little Moreton today, you first walk through the Gatehouse in the south range, which dates back to the 1560s. The decoration here is a curious mix of old and, at the time, new: although there are the interweaving vines, cable mouldings and trefoils common to much earlier buildings, the decoration also reveals the influence of Italian Renaissance design that was fashionable across Europe in the 15th century such as the 'anticke work' over the outer door and the awkwardly-carved warriors that stand either side of the entrance.

Little Moreton's glass

30,000 leaded panes (known as quarries) pattern the windows at Little Moreton Hall, complementing the exquisitely moulded timbers in which they are set, with each group showing a different arrangement of triangles, rectangles, diamonds, circles, squares and lozenges.

Much of the original glass has, of course, been lost over the centuries, with the house itself partly to blame. The wooden structure continually moves and can cause the lead holding the glass to open up so that the panes fall out. The lead, too, has deteriorated over time (a process not helped by pollution). Although much of the glass today is Victorian and quite plain, at its height the windows at Little Moreton Hall might have been quite colourful, perhaps featuring the various coats of arms associated with the Moretons.

Left **A carved greyhound on the corner of the porch leading into the Great Hall**

Right **Detail of the leaded windows in the Gallery Chamber**

Far right **The stained glass window in the Great Parlour**

Making Tudor glass

During the 15th and 16th centuries, glass was made by hand. It was blown using the two most successful glass-making techniques of the time: crown glass and cylinder blown sheet glass. The imperfections inherent in these techniques, which left traces of copper, iron or manganese, lend these original panes an iridescent quality. It also led to glass that was too fragile to be cut by a diamond point. Instead, it was cleaved into shape using a hot iron. Although we can't say for sure where Little Moreton's glass was made, we know that by 1589 there were 15 glass factories in England, the nearest being at Bishop's Wood, Eccleshall and on Cannock Chase in Staffordshire. An archaeological dig also revealed a glass-making site near Biddulph Old Hall, just four miles away, and it is possible that itinerant smiths travelled to the area to supply the glass here.

Until the 1570s, glass was rare and remained a luxury even to the well-off – so much so that, if you moved, you would probably take your glass with you.

The Courtyard

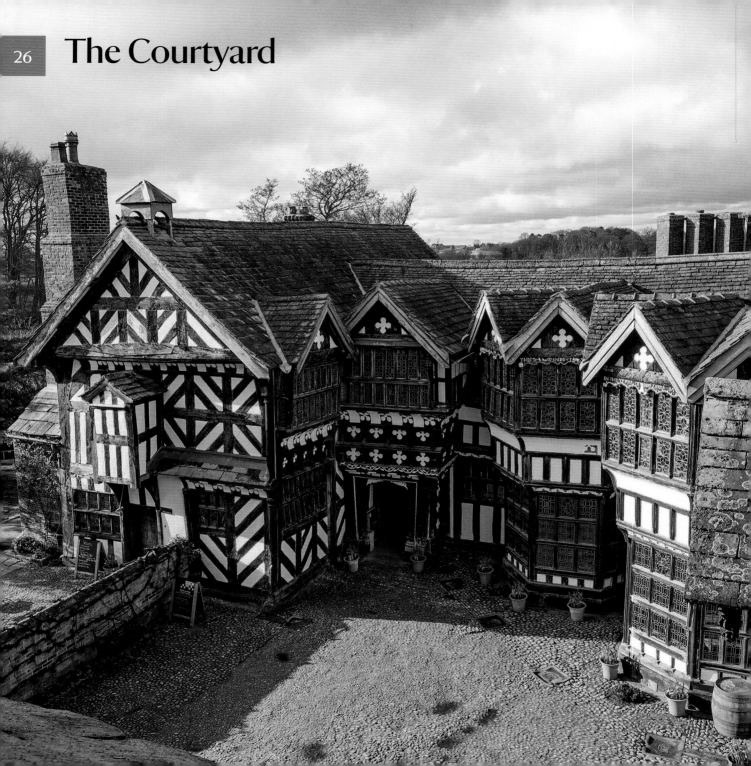

The Hall's enclosed courtyard gives a sense of both the complexity of the building's design and also some of its pragmatism. On the porch in the corner and on the north-west cross wing the carvings are wonderfully decorative, with quatrefoils (resembling four-leaf clovers) carved out of solid wood, twisted columns and chamfered pilasters, greyhounds and a wolf's head (which are also seen on the Moreton's shield and crest respectively), and carved dragons all vying for attention. The latter alludes to the Welsh dragon that appeared on the royal coat of arms under the Tudor monarchy. The bay windows are similarly ambitious, the initials and names carved into them announcing they were built by the carpenter Richard Dale in 1559.

Prepared for a close-up

In early Tudor times, courtyards like this acted as a kind of halfway point between the house and the outside world, allowing inhabitants to watch for arrivals and departures, and ensuring that visitors could closely view (and thus appreciate) the design of the buildings ranged around. So it's not for nothing that the walls and windows facing onto the courtyard are so highly decorative: they were designed to look impressive at close quarters.

Left A view across the courtyard to the Great Parlour's bay windows

Right A carved warrior on the doorway on the courtyard side of the south range

What was once here?

Although today Little Moreton Hall appears relatively compact, the land and buildings around it were once more complex. The estate took in farmland, two corn mills, a bloomery – where iron was smelted – and even ponds used as fish farms.

The house may have been surrounded by other buildings. There are postholes in the orchard and medieval wall tiles were found elsewhere on the site, suggesting there were once earlier houses in the area. However, we don't know whether these were razed to accommodate the new Hall as we see it now.

Another clue as to how the house was once structured comes in the form of the decoration within the courtyard. To the right of the small brick wall outside the Tea Room, where the family's living quarters once would have been the decoration is rich and elaborate but to the left, it is plainer. This suggests that there were once two courtyards: the main one, and a more functional service courtyard, screened off from the activities of the Hall itself and thus only deserving of more basic design.

Chimney stacks
The Tea Rooms
The Brewhouse

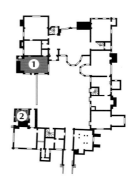

Chimney stacks

There is ongoing debate around Little Moreton's chimneys, in particular their age. Chimneys didn't become commonplace in Tudor house building until the end of the 16th century, which would suggest the early 16th-century Hall was originally built without chimneys. Yet evidence points otherwise. First, there was once a marl pit on the estate; this is where clay was extracted, meaning bricks could have been made on site. The family's bloomery also tells us they had the fuel needed to fire such bricks. Second, the Great Parlour chimney must predate Elizabeth I's death in 1603 because the overmantel bears her coat of arms. Third, the glass in the window in the Great Hall chimney was being replaced in 1660, so the chimney must be older than that.

Finally, early house taxes rested on the number of hearths a house contained (in 1664, Edward Moreton was taxed for 15). Consequently less well-off families simply would not have been able to afford them. So with chimneys as much status symbols as glass in windows (see page 25), they were probably an early priority for the status-conscious Moretons.

All these clues point to the fact that the chimneys were likely installed early on in the Hall's life.

How many ovens?

Today, the brewhouse contains the public toilets, but the brick-fronted bread oven is still there. The internal bricks possibly date from the 17th century and the bull-nosed brickwork over the oven door (and the iron door itself) from the 19th. The protruding face was probably added later.

But there are also two arched recesses above the ladies' toilet sink, leading many to question how many ovens Little Moreton Hall had: one, two or three? In fact, we suspect that the block's original oven was housed in the left-hand alcove before being usurped by the oven with the 19th-century face. As for the recess on the right-hand side, its shape suggests that it wasn't an oven at all. But as to what it was – we really don't know.

Left Queen Elizabeth's coat of arms on the chimney overmantel in the Great Parlour, which has helped us date the chimney

1 The Tea Rooms

Once the likely site of the Tudor kitchens, and later the farm tenants' kitchen, stuffed with the furniture of a typical Victorian farmhouse, today's Tea Rooms have long been the place visitors head to for a bite to eat.

Here, the Dale family made the teas that were served in the Great Parlour and, if it was busy, the Great Hall. There continues to be a bakery on site, with 80% of our food made on the premises. Note the bell tower above the doorway: it was once used to call people together for prayer or farm workers in for lunch, and other such occasions.

2 The Brewhouse

The block that now houses the ladies' and gents' toilets once served as a brewhouse, bakehouse and a place to wash clothes. It made sense to combine the three, as they had similar needs: brewing and washing required lots of hot and cold water (and the brew coppers were ideal for washing clothes), while brewing and baking required fermentation (the yeasty liquid worked out of beer casks was reused to raise bread). And although not everyone approved of the arrangement, especially the brewers, it was at least a cost-effective means of production.

Left The east wall of the house, showing a chimney breast which serves several rooms

Above The Tea Rooms as they were in 1893

The Great Hall

This room is one of the oldest parts of Little Moreton Hall, dating from c.1504–1508. It was then a simple room used for complicated purposes, including protection, justice, family, hospitality, and much more. Its earth floor would have been covered with rushes, with an open hearth set beneath a smoke canopy in the middle of the room.

Screens passage

Entrance to the Great Hall is via a screens passage, a wooden construction added in 1546 and designed as a form of draught-stopper. The now-missing wooden screens once provided a buffer between the door and the hall and services on the left.

The Gallery

Opposite the porch door, through a small door, is a spiral staircase that leads to the gallery over the screens passage (now a private area). Originally open to the Great Hall (and a spot for minstrels (musicians) to play to those gathered below), the Gallery led to the Moreton family's original private rooms, three rooms with fireplaces, garderobes and an impressively arch-braced roof with cusped wind-braces.

Above Details on the porch leading to the Great Hall

Left The movable screen at Rufford Old Hall, Lancashire (also National Trust) gives some idea of what the one at Little Moreton Hall might have looked like

Opposite The Great Hall as it appears today; the outline of the doorway at first floor (gallery) level can still be seen

Changing times

Under the Tudors, the focus of domestic life gradually shifted from the Great Hall towards smaller, more private rooms. In 1559, William Moreton II modernised the house, refurbishing the Great Parlour and putting in a new floor above the Great Hall. (This was removed before 1807, though the sawn-off remnants of the beams that supported it can be seen halfway up the east wall, above the doorway.) The two bay windows were also installed, designed to allow light into both floors.

The carpenter

Richard Dale was key to the building of Little Moreton Hall. A craftsman of exceptional skill and ability, he did everything from choosing trees for timber to making scale drawings. As well as creating the bay windows that bear his inscription, Dale was most likely employed by William Moreton II to build the south range; the beams here are similar to his work in the Great Hall and Great Parlour.

Glass, tables and pewter

The windows here were elaborately designed, with the surviving stained sections bearing the coat of arms belonging to the Brereton family (see page 14). The 500-year-old table is actually a board that sits loose on top of trestles; it is from these earliest 'board' tables that many common words and phrases derive: cupboards (as cups would once have been stored on trestle tables), board games, bed and board and so on. The pewter tableware is mostly 18th-century, though some pieces may be those mentioned in a 1654 inventory.

Highs and lows

In the early 16th century, households were still organised as they had been since medieval times, family and servants living and working together. But status was underlined by how rooms were used, and what they were called. So buildings were understood in terms of high and low ends and, as time went on, this changed to the difference between upper floor rooms (more significant) and ground floor ones (less so). This too began to change, as under Elizabeth I it became important to underline status via privacy. Master and servant became divided and rooms were no longer shared.

Above **Details from the Great Hall**

Right **Carpenter Richard Dale's inscription on the** exterior of the Great Parlour's bay windows, which can be seen from the courtyard

The Little Parlour

In 1976, a hidden layer to this room was revealed. For the first four decades that the National Trust cared for Little Moreton Hall, this diminutive room was remarkable only for its age, its views across the garden and the fact that, with Georgian windows and a floor that dates to 1956, it is the most modernised room in the house. But in 1976 a discovery was made. Hidden behind the wood panelling was elaborate decoration, painted on the plaster, and in places on paper which was pasted onto the wall. This can still be seen today.

Biblical scenes and a detailed frieze sandwiched between ornamental borders sit above fairly crudely drawn panels whose centres are colourfully decorated in alternate red and green, with grained and marbled effects. The fashion for such paintwork only lasted for around forty years (from c.1570 to 1610); as at Little Moreton, such painted scenes were often covered up by wooden panels, to be rediscovered centuries later.

Above A view of the Little Parlour, including the uncovered 16th-century panelling

The detail

The frieze contains the Moretons' wolf's head crest and the initial 'I' for John Moreton (who died in 1598), while the biblical scenes depict the story of Susanna and the Elders from the Apocrypha (see boxout). Black lettered inscriptions either side of the paintings tell this biblical story.

Panels such as these were commonplace in wealthy homes as a sign of their occupants' faith and education – the establishment of the Church of England under Elizabeth I, the increasing availability of an English language Bible, and the shaking off of many of the rituals that surrounded the Catholic faith encouraged the literate to study the teachings of Christ themselves. So while biblical scenes were being whitewashed over in churches, they were found inside private homes more often. Susanna and the Elders was just such a tale.

In the Long Gallery, other Protestant creeds, namely the virtues of hard work and the power of knowledge over superstition, can be found (see pages 46–47).

Below Detail of the painted panelling discovered beneath the panelling – the Moretons' wolf's head can be seen on these, suggesting this was designed especially for the family

The story of Susanna and the Elders

Susanna was the beautiful wife of a wealthy citizen of Babylon, Joachim. One day, two of Joachim's business associates – a pair of elderly judges – visited his house and spied his wife bathing in the garden. As she headed back into the house, they accosted her, threatening that if she didn't sleep with them they would claim she'd been meeting her lover in the garden. She refused, and they brought her to trial for adultery. With Susanna about to be stoned to death, a young man called Daniel interceded. He demanded the men be questioned separately to establish the true facts of the case. Their stories unravelled and they were proven to be liars; Susanna was freed and the judges were condemned to death.

The Great Parlour
The Activity Room
The Exhibition Room

1 The Great Parlour

This wonderfully, heavily wood-panelled room gets its stature largely – we think – from the work of the carpenter, Richard Dale; the bay window, the wood panels and the elaborately moulded ceiling beams, similar to those in the Great Hall, are all likely to have been made at his hand during the 1559 alterations to the house. But that's not all that's interesting about a room that was, as curious as it now sounds, variously used as a kitchen and for domestic chores by later generations of Moretons.

Stained glass

The glass in the windows opposite the bay is some of the finest that survives, with some of it dating to the 16th century. The left-hand window depicts a greyhound courant, the shield of the Moretons (in heraldry, 'courant' refers to the depiction of a running animal with its legs extended). The right-hand window displays the family's wolf's head crest, a panel with the initials W.M. (for William Moreton II) – and a visual joke on the name Moreton. The wolf's open mouth or 'maw' sounds similar to 'More' and 'tun' is another word for barrel, sounding similar to 'ton'. So 'Maw-tun' becomes 'More-ton' in the pun-laden visual language of heraldry.

Fireplace

The fireplace is mid-18th century, but the overmantel is original and bears the royal arms belonging to Elizabeth I. Given that Parliamentarian soldiers were based here during the Civil War for various short periods of time, we can only assume Elizabeth's coat of arms survived by being hastily covered up by the Royalist Moretons – but we do not know for certain that this was the case.

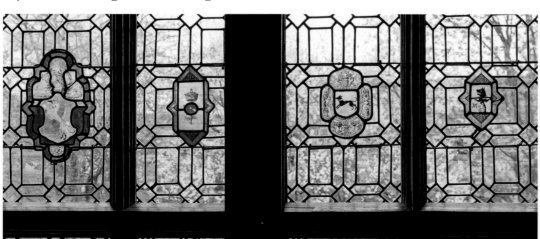

Furniture

This room contains two pieces of original furniture: the 16th-century octagonal table, probably designed to sit in one of the Hall's bay windows, and the 'cupborde of boxes' mentioned in the 1599 inventory. This 25-drawer oak cabinet, hidden behind a panelled facade was most likely used for storing documents. It is exquisitely crafted, with each drawer corresponding exactly (and only) to its specific slot.

2 The Activity Room

Built after the north range, this room's purpose during the Moretons' time is unclear. Later, when Ann Dale was the tenant here, this and the Exhibition Room next door were used as the cottage for a farm worker and his wife.

3 The Exhibition Room

After William Moreton III's death, his children split the house into semi-self-contained flats. This room was probably Ann Moreton's kitchen (she lived in the Chapel Chamber above).

A pet for all seasons
Leaving the Exhibition Room for the courtyard and turning back to the Chapel, you may notice a small alcove in the wall. This is a Victorian dog kennel.

Left A view of the Great Parlour including the 'cupborde of boxes'

Far left A selection of stained glass crests, including the Moretons'

The Chapel

This 500-year-old chapel is a rare thing indeed: an example of a domestic chapel that survived the Reformation more or less intact.

Although the chancel was added later (as part of an extension), all of it probably still dates to the early 16th century. It was and remains a holy space. Its layout runs along an east-west axis, the altar at the east end allowing the congregation to face Jerusalem. Its separate entrance (directly from the Courtyard), independence from other rooms and its continuing Sunday services all underline its sacred status. Services are held during the summer months; check ahead for details.

Decoration

Before the Reformation, the furnishings within the Chapel would have been sumptuous, with plate, vestments, altar furnishings, hangings and panel paintings all designed to reflect the Moretons' spirituality and, of course, their wealth and social standing. Such decorations disappeared during the Reformation so the surviving paintings you can see probably date later, from the 1580s. They are similar in style to those found in the Little Parlour, framed with the arabesques and motifs characteristic of the Italian Renaissance.

Fall and rise

The Chapel suffered decades of neglect after the Moretons began renting out the Hall; it was deconsecrated (though we're not sure when) and eventually became a storeroom. It was only in 1893, when Elizabeth Moreton inherited the house, that it was restored and reconsecrated, and her work was continued by her cousin, Bishop Abraham (see pages 56–57). Amongst other restorations, the Bishop's work included installing the stained glass in 1938, his parting gift to a house he was about to hand over to the National Trust. Designed by Gerald Smith, the glass reflects the previous ministry of the Bishop in the Derby and Lichfield dioceses.

Above The Chapel, including the chancel screen

Left A view of the altar and stained glass window and wall inscriptions

'He led me across the courtyard to a doorway, which I had thought was an entrance to the coal cellar, and sure enough there was a coal cellar, for what had once been the ante-chapel was converted into a depot for coals and rubbish.'

The artist James West recalling a visit to Little Moreton's Chapel in 1847

An artistic interpretation

When the artist James West visited Little Moreton in 1847, he drew an interlocking pattern identical to that in the midway frieze in the Little Parlour, which he stuck into the section of his notebook marked 'Ornaments on the beams of the Chapel'. The stable groom had shown him into the Chapel and, although part of it was being used to store coal, he was still able to complete detailed sketches of the wall texts. He had a professional interest in them, having just finished the decoration of a chapel at nearby Crewe Hall.

The Chapel Chamber
The Great Chamber
The Bridge Chamber

1 The Chapel Chamber

Built at the same time as the Chapel below, this room served as Ann Moreton's bedroom in the 17th century, with her maid staying in the room next door. Ann had a grand bedstead with 'five blew curtaynes and a vallence', with a trundle bed beneath, another bed with two red curtains and a 'canabye' (canopy), plus a little table. A great press (wardrobe) stood against the wall with a cupboard at the end of it. The west-facing window was curtained, probably to keep out the sun, and a large chest was underneath. The ceiling, meanwhile, was put in during the late 16th century, having previously been open to the arch-braced roof trusses. Some time at the beginning of the 16th century, one of

these arch braces was removed to enable a squint (a rectangular hole punched into the east wall) to be installed, as it would have been in the way; the mortice hole can still be seen in the west wall.

A religious room?

We call this room the Chapel Chamber simply because it was once connected to the Chapel below via the squint, though it may have been used by the family for religious purposes. The squint would have enabled the family to observe and even take part in services being conducted in the Chapel below. If that was the case, it must have only been a short-term use: the room was built in around 1508 without the squint, and the wall paintings in

Below An archive view of the Chapel Chamber. The squint would have been the large horizontal section of plaster on the left

the Chapel that now cover it date from around the 1580s, so it must have been blocked up about this time.

The presence of the squint makes this room one of the most significant in the house, due to its connection to the Chapel below; belief in God was a central part of Tudor life to such an extent that it is now hard for us to grasp quite how important this was.

2 The Great Chamber

This was once called the Joiner's Chamber, and was possibly part of Philip Moreton's living quarters in the 1640s, when he moved back to Little Moreton to look after the property and act as his brother Edward's agent. Afterwards his books were kept in a closet here.

The massive carved consoles, one tree-ring-dated to around 1660, were used for both decoration and support – they helped take some of the load of the unstable Long Gallery. The panelled partition was added later, again to help support the Gallery above.

Floor and fire

Fire was an ever-present threat to timber-framed buildings. Large-scale blazes that razed buildings, streets and even towns were commonplace; in 1583, Nantwich (in Cheshire, about 16 miles from Little Moreton Hall) suffered a fire so devastating that Elizabeth I made a personal contribution to its rebuilding. It's not surprising, then, that the Tudors did all they could to reduce the risk – with the lime-ash flooring used at Little Moreton a good example. Flexible, light and fireproof, it, along with the plaster infill between timbers, created a barrier against fire.

3 The Bridge Chamber

Adjoining the Great Chamber, this room was also probably used by Philip Moreton. In the 1654 inventory, it was recorded as holding a bed and a little table.

Left The south corner of the Great Chamber

Above The west window and Great Chamber, as viewed from the Bridge Chamber

The South Chamber
The Brewhouse Chamber

1 The South Chamber

Little is known about the South Chamber, although its functional, roughly finished ceiling beams suggest it was one of Little Moreton's less important rooms. The south and west windows were blocked up (the former opened by Bishop Abraham and the latter by Elizabeth Moreton in 1893), but we're not sure why. We do know, however, that this room was once recorded as 'Mr Booth's Chamber', referring to Jack Booth of Tremlowe, the cousin of William Moreton III, who was living with the family when Civil War broke out in 1642. The fact that this was his room explains the elaborately panelled fireplace, and while the 1654 inventory mentions only basic furnishings – two bedsteads and a grate – Jack's own things wouldn't have been listed so it was probably much more comfortably laid out.

Make yourself comfortable
The replica Tudor tester bed in this room, with a solid oak frame, wool canopy and drapes, may be similar to that once slept in by Jack Booth. A feather mattress is stacked on top of a straw one, with ropes beneath which would regularly be pulled tight to keep the bed comfortable.

Right **The Brewhouse Chamber**

Below **The South Chamber, including the replica Tudor bed**

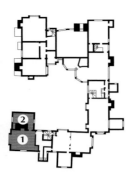

2 The Brewhouse Chamber

This is another functional room, part of a block built in the 17th century for the brewhouse and bakehouse below. We're not sure what the wooden planked structure in the corner was for; experts tell us it wasn't used as part of the brewing process, although the room itself could have been used for storage or as somewhere for servants to sleep. Storerooms often doubled up as servants' rooms and, given that brewing was a 24-hour process, it makes sense that servants could have grabbed forty winks here, using a hatch in the ceiling of the brewhouse below for easy access. The floor as we see it now may not have existed at this height, or even at all.

Above Detail of a beam in the South Chamber

Towers and toilets

Garderobes were typical toilets for the wealthier Tudor: earth closets that led directly outside, the effluent either collected for fertiliser or deposited into the moat.

The name garderobe literally translates as guarding one's robes – it is thought to come from the practice of hanging clothes inside the closet, as Tudors believed the ammonia from urine would kill moths that had taken a fancy to a piece of apparel.

At Little Moreton, there is a garderobe tower between the South Chamber and the Great Chamber whose two closets have their original seats; there are two more below (though not directly – they are offset in front of the first floor ones to prevent accidents!).

The Long Gallery

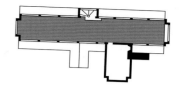

Perched precariously atop the first floor, it is the Long Gallery that gives this house so much of its character.

Yet for all its dramatic shape and size, the Long Gallery has also almost been Little Moreton's downfall – as it has led to major structural problems and repairs that generations of Moretons have struggled to contain.

What went wrong?

Most timber-framed houses were built one floor at a time, with the ceiling of one forming the floor of the other (see pages 8–9). So the Long Gallery should have been positioned directly over the frame underneath but it is much narrower (just over 3.5 metres (12 feet) wide as opposed to the 6-metre (20 foot) width of the Great and South Chambers below). It has no direct support and, to make matters worse, the roof is covered with enormously heavy grit-stone slabs. Yet the decision to build the Long Gallery in this way may have been deliberate. While it should have been as wide as the rooms below, a narrower room appeared to be much longer. In other words, its narrowness made it look more dramatic – or at least it did, until the cracks began to show.

Left The east end of the Long Gallery

Making amends

Even shortly after it was built, the Moretons had to take action to repair the Long Gallery. Records show Philip Moreton measuring up the roof for repair work in 1658. This work only did so much, though, and in the 1890s Elizabeth Moreton inserted iron tie-rods (see page 56). But even that wasn't enough. In 1979, some steel work was done, which you can see on the north wall above the door to the stairs. Then in 1990–1, a steel frame was inserted, the majority of the front of the house was taken off and many windows were replaced in structural repairs that took 16 months to complete.

Plasterwork

The painted plasterwork here is remarkable. Destiny and Fortune stand proud at either end, echoing a design taken from the 1556 edition of *The Castle of Knowledge*, a treatise written by the mathematician Robert Recorde, who invented the 'equals' sign.

What was it for?

In the Elizabethan era, it was fashionable for manor houses to contain a long, narrow hall, a room used daily for exercise and games, and in 1977 we found a tennis ball in this Long Gallery. Made of Italian leather and filled with moss or feathers, the Wimbledon Lawn Tennis Museum dated it to the early 17th century. More balls were discovered during the 1990–1 renovations. The 1654 inventory also lists only a few items of furniture, mainly chairs, stools and 'one safe', a type of hanging cupboard for food.

Above A close-up of the plasterwork in the Long Gallery

Left The front cover of *The Castle of Knowledge*, the book from which the designs for the striking plasterwork pictures were taken

Right An exterior view of the South Chamber, with the Long Gallery windows above

When was it built?

There is an ongoing debate as to when the Long Gallery was actually built. The south range was built in the early 1560s, but experts argue that such a date would be unusually early for this type of room in this region. It certainly wasn't part of the original design of William Moreton II and Richard Dale's south range either, because it is imperfectly jointed to and loaded onto the first-floor ceiling joists. Yet it wasn't a complete afterthought; the stairwell has been dendro-dated to 1560–2 and the newell post is a single section of wood that stretches from the ground floor all the way to the top of the building, suggesting that the three floors *were* built together. Meanwhile, there's no sign of roof trusses having been removed from above first floor level, and the consistent bracing and window moulding indicate that while they may not have been started together, all three floors were at least finished at the same time.

Taking a design from a book was the norm for Tudor plasterwork, but taking a design from a book printed in English was much more unusual. Whoever translated the design from printed page to plaster, however, made a few mistakes. Fortune should hold a string attached to the Wheel of Fortune; instead, her arm is simply held aloft. The mottos aren't quite right either: Robert Recorde's 'The sphere of destinye whose governour is knowledge' here becomes 'The speare of destinye whose ruler is knowledge'. It probably didn't matter, as the words still underlined the Protestant belief that individual striving and knowledge determined one's destiny, and chime perfectly with an age that boasted numerous intellectual achievements including developments in astronomy from Copernicus and Galileo, and a leap in literacy and printing.

The Gallery Chamber

Walk into this room and you may well be struck by the sense that the heavily decorated fireplace that dominates this small space is askew.

It's not. The overmantel (above a fireplace mantel) is actually level; it's the rest of the room, or more accurately the floor, that is sloping so badly. Although it is stable now, this section of the house, which includes the Gatehouse below and was built at the same time as the Long Gallery, had to be pinned back to the front of the house during the repairs in the 1990s.

Still, for all its disorientating flooring, this cosy room was once the place you'd retire to if the fun and games of the Long Gallery proved too much. It later became a bedroom (furnished in the same way as the Bridge Chamber directly below) with a curtained and carved bed, and green cloth-covered chair, stool and cupboard.

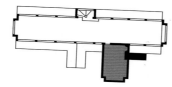

Left The fireplace in the Gallery Chamber; the photo gives some sense of the illusion of the sloping floor

Far left A detail of the leaded windows

The fireplace decorations

As with the décor next door and in the Little Parlour, the plasterwork underlines Protestant values: Justice standing with her scales, Prudence with an open book. Once brightly painted and featuring mythical sea creatures, the central panel contains the Moreton arms, quartered by the cross of the Macclesfield family – a celebration of the prudent marriage in 1329 of John de Moreton to Margaret, the co-heiress to the estate of John de Macclesfield.

The Garden and Estate

Like the rest of Little Moreton Hall, much of what we know about the garden is based on fragmentary records, as well as what we know about Elizabethan gardens.

Elizabethan gardens began to combine practical spaces for the growing of fruit, vegetables and herbs with more decorative pleasure gardens, though the property archives give little evidence for how the garden looked before the 17th century, but an archaeological dig in 2009 shows evidence of an earlier building under the current lawned area of the garden.

Philip's Garden

The earliest evidence for the garden is a 17th-century set of accounts that notes the costs of a gardener, seeds and the putting in of an apple tree, but when Philip Moreton took over the estate in the mid-17th century, he kept more meticulous records. The garden we find in his notebooks occupies the same location as today's, and was probably surrounded by a paling fence whose hooks were used for espaliered plum and bergamot pear trees. Underneath, Philip planted a border with 29 'collyflowers', while the rest of the garden was typically 17th-century: divided into quarters, and the quarters further divided into beds where vegetables, flowers and herbs such as sweet marjoram were grown. There were fruit trees, too, with a nursery sheltering saplings until they could be planted in the orchard. Philip also mentions another nursery 'att side of the ould Dogkennell' planted with '30 slipps of the dwarf apple', while against the brewhouse wall a border was dug in 1668 and an 'Apricock tree' planted.

The moat

We think the moat was originally built in the 13th or 14th century around another now non-existent house. At that time, moats were generally built as a status symbol, rather than for military defence, and it was possibly more likely to be used to keep animals, rather than people, out. In the Tudor era, it was probably – along with other stew (fish) ponds on the estate – used as a kind of fish farm. Now it is home to more dramatic-looking fish, such as the golden orfe, which were introduced by the National Trust.

The mount

Although the mount (or 'mound') is one of the garden's main features, there are no known documents that tell us its precise history. It was probably created in the 16th century to act as a vantage point from which to view the geometric beds of a knot garden or the surrounding countryside. One of two, the second can be found outside the moat; it lent its name to the Mount Yard, a grassy area next to which lay the 'ould cowfield' where cows were kept for milking.

The back view

The house wasn't always set so far back from the main road. Before the A34 was built, the road came much closer, cutting across what is now the car park and going up past the back of the Hall towards Great Moreton. This explains why the back of the house is so decorative, and, for example, why the stonework on the east side of the moat bridge includes the Moreton crest – it is likely that visitors approached the front of the house from the opposite side of the bridge to today. Clearly visible to passing traffic, the back of Little Moreton Hall – just like the front – was designed to impress.

Above Cows in the moat of Little Moreton Hall, 1893

Opposite *Little Moreton from the South East* by George Theaker, 1886

Around the garden: Tudor plants

In the Tudor period, plants were much more than just decorative items: many were used for help around the home. The purpose of others was less practical, instead rooted more in the folklore and symbolism of the period. You can see some of the plants they used growing in the gardens at Little Moreton today.

Culinary herbs and vegetables

Used for flavouring foods from simple stews to expensive meats, herbs were an important part of the garden for rich and poor alike. Vegetables, on the other hand, were more commonly eaten by poorer Tudors, with the rich preferring meat.

Skirret

Many of the herbs and vegetables that the Tudors used are still common today, for example carrots, artichokes, cucumbers, mint, sage, parsley, fennel and thyme. Others are less familiar, such as the skirret; similar to a very sweet parsnip, its fleshy white roots can be roasted and these were a favourite of King Henry VIII.

Harvesting peas and beans

Broad beans were used by the lower orders and often dried for winter use together with peas, which could be used in dishes such as pease pottage, a light yellow, savoury pudding that is similar in texture to hummus (it's also sometimes known as pease pudding).

Left *Herball*, or *Generall Histories of Plantes* by John Gerard was published in 1597. At 1480 pages it contained more than 1,000 species and became the first plant catalogue. It was the most widely circulated botany book in English in the 17th century and remains a popular resource for those interested in plant remedies

Below The skirret has an inedible woody core; it should be removed before cooking as it is difficult to do so after

Household plants

Plants had a variety of household uses. The Tudor botanist and herbalist John Gerard advised keeping bay leaves in flour to ward off weevils, making a tick and flea repellant by mixing together rosemary, pennyroyal and mint, or deodorising boots by combining equal quantities of ground rosemary, lemonbalm and peppermint and placing these inside.

Strewing herbs

Acting as a disinfectant and medieval air freshener, sweet-smelling plants such as water mint, rosemary and lavender were scattered over floors; this mixture continued to be used up until about the 18th century. Elizabeth I's favourite was said to be meadowsweet.

Love poseys

Love poseys may be left or given to a sweetheart, and flowers were selected for their particular significance. So a posey might contain daisies for innocence, honeysuckle for devotion, a red rose for love, ivy for fidelity, violet for faithfulness or modesty, and of course forget-me-nots.

Above left to right
Also known as 'bouncing bet', soapwart is part of the carnation family

Popular uses of chamomile today include treating hay fever, inflammation, muscle spasms and insomnia

Wild strawberries are still used in homeopathic medicines today, such as using the leaves as an astringent for sore throats, cuts, burns and bruises

Right Making soapballs from natural resources

Medicinal plants

From woodruff being put into wine as it was considered good for the heart and liver, to wild strawberry leaves being used to strengthen 'gummes and festeneth the teeth', the Tudors believed many plants had health benefits and herbs were often dried and distilled for medicinal use.

Tussey musseys

These posies of flowers and herbs were carried by Tudors, who thought they would protect people from disease – particularly the plague. The smell certainly disguised some of the less pleasant odours you might experience in a Tudor house. The bouquet contained any available plants with a sweet, strong smell, such as mint, lavender, soapwort flowers, viola and violets. The lower orders would use plants growing freely in the hedgerows.

The garden and estate today

The Knot Garden

There are few – if any – surviving Elizabethan knot gardens – these labour-intensive gardens, trimmed annually by hand and leveled by eye, fell out of fashion during Charles II's reign – so we have based the design of ours on a book called the *Complete English Gardener* by Leonard Meager (1670). The design also echoes the quatrefoil pattern on the house.

The garden was laid out in 1972 and takes the form of an 'open knot', with fine gravel (rather than plants) laid between sections of hedge. Nowadays we use slow growing box for the garden, but the Tudors probably used a different type of evergreen plant. Our gardener still uses the traditional method of hand-cutting to maintain the garden, a task on which he spends 80 hours a year.

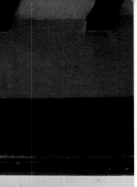

The yews

The yew pyramids inside the knot garden illustrate how Renaissance design influenced fashionable English homes during the Tudor period, while the yew tunnel that runs along one side created a sheltered walkway that echoed the idea of the Long Gallery – a more private space within which the family could exercise and talk.

The estate

Little Moreton Hall's estate was once extensive: covering 550 hectares (1,360 acres), it generated enough income to help the Moretons build the Hall – and to keep building it for the best part of a century. The Moretons were so successful in part because they were apparently unafraid of trying their hand at different things. From the late 15th century they owned a water-powered bloomsmithy (a furnace used for smelting iron) as well as two corn mills, and several stew pools, which were used to breed fish such as carp and tench, an important part of the Tudor diet. By the 17th century they also had a share in a coal pit. Towards the end of the 18th century, the bloomery pool had partly silted up and was being used as a fish pond, as were the corn mill pools. The mills themselves had fallen into disrepair, with the bulk of the estate income at this point coming from selling timber and fish from the estate, and the farm and cottage rents.

Opposite Tudors found the inspiration for knot gardens in Italy; they liked the idea of geometry and proportion

Left Looking across the bridge from the Gatehouse porch and to the farmland beyond

Above right A bird's eye view of Little Moreton Hall and the wider estate, by an unknown artist

What happened to the farm?

The farm adjacent to Little Moreton Hall, and whose 16th-century cruick barn can be seen through the east windows of the Great Parlour, was once part of a complex that included a stable, 'oxehouse', 'wainhouse' and a dovecot. Today it is owned by descendants of the Abraham family, who inherited Little Moreton Hall in the 20th century (see pages 56-7).

Saving Little Moreton

The first conservator of Little Moreton Hall was a member of the Moreton family, Elizabeth Moreton, who was followed by her second cousin, Charles Thomas Abraham.

Elizabeth Moreton (1821–1912)

Where once the decay of Little Moreton Hall had felt romantic (see pages 20–21), by the late 19th century it threatened to be terminal – and so it may have been had Elizabeth Moreton not inherited the house in 1892. Wealthy and possessed of strong religious and moral conviction, this Sister of the Community of St John the Baptist at Clewer was determined to save a house that she inherited relatively late in her life. It was she who began the long process of saving Little Moreton from collapse, installing metal tie-rods in the Long Gallery and Gallery Chamber – thus stabilising the whole of the

south range – as well as the metal ties and post in the Chapel. She restored the Chapel too, and also considered the long-term future of the house: in the same year she inherited it, she wrote to her cousin, Charles Thomas Abraham (also known as Bishop Abraham), and asked him to become her heir. There was only one condition to Elizabeth's bequest: that Little Moreton was never sold.

Above The tie rods Elizabeth inserted in the long gallery can be seen here going across the width of the room

Left Sister Elizabeth Moreton (sitting). We think this photo was taken in the late 1860s, before she inherited Little Moreton Hall from her sister, Annabella

Charles Thomas Abraham (Bishop Abraham) (c.1858–1945)

Elizabeth made a wise choice when she chose her cousin, as Charles was as committed to Little Moreton's restoration as she was. After Elizabeth's death, he turned to specialists for support. A Derby-based architect, a Mr Thompson, worked on the Hall's repair. Instead of hiring a building firm, he hired an experienced carpenter to carry out the works gradually. In March 1928, in a report written for the Society for the Protection of Ancient Buildings, their then chief architect praised the quality of the men's work.

Eventually, though, Charles realised that the scale of restoration was beyond his means and, in 1937, he offered the Hall to the National Trust. A public appeal raised enough money to cover various costs – including the £1,000 needed for immediate structural repairs – and in 1938, Little Moreton Hall was handed over to the Trust. The Hall had an owner unconnected to the Moreton family for the first time in its history.

'Sister Elizabeth lavished I fancy far more than all the income on its stability and maintenance, rescued, visited and loved every corner.'

Bishop Abraham, writing in his notebook in 1937

Above The interior of the Great Hall in 1893, not long after Elizabeth inherited the Hall

Right Bishop Abraham in 1910 (photographer unknown)

How is it still standing?

At the beginning of this book, we mentioned that the most-asked question about Little Moreton Hall is how it remains standing. The answer is deceptively simple: centuries of conservation and structural repair, first by the Moretons and later by the National Trust.

Constant monitoring

Seasonal movement is part of the life of all wooden-frame buildings, and usually any damage is easily repaired. We have to constantly monitor the movement at Little Moreton Hall, checking its overall condition and undertaking a full survey every five years. Laser monitors help us assess how much the building has moved, and we also measure cracks and replace sections of timber. We also do battle with death watch beetle and woodworm, and in rooms such as the Little Parlour, use special lights, humidity sensors and constant low heat to preserve fragile interiors.

Tudor techniques

Wherever possible we use the same material that the Tudors would have, and retain as much as we can of what already exists. For example, when the lime-ash floor in the Great Chamber needed replacing in 2002 we mixed wood ash, lime and gypsum, along with ground-up sections of the old floor, using a retardant to counter the fact that contemporary gypsum sets faster than its Tudor counterpart. This mixture was then packed between the original 400-year-old oak laths and joists.

Trial and error

The Tudors didn't leave us any recipe books, and so not all our period-sympathetic repairs turn out quite as we expect; the lime-ash floor in the Chapel Chamber has been patched with concrete, a material we would not use today because it does not flex seasonally like the wood of the building's frame. The renewal of the lime-ash floor in the Gallery Chamber in 1991 also proved an interesting experiment; we were aiming for a hard-wearing floor to cope with the footfall of our 80,000 annual visitors. However it was a bit too rigid and didn't move with the house, so started to damage the wall panelling. This meant we had to chip it away from the edge of the panels to allow for movement.

The benefits of benign neglect

The years of neglect that Little Moreton suffered may have saved it from more disastrous attempts at restoration. The Victorians often fudged (well-meaning) attempts at restoration – tending to put back what they thought should be there, rather than what actually existed – but because money was so tight at Little Moreton, the family adopted a more pragmatic policy of patching, filling and supporting what was there – which chimes with the much more sympathetic way that the National Trust (and many other organisations) look after historic properties today.

Left Scaffolding on the south range when undergoing a paint job; this happens about every five years

Opposite Conservation in action in the Great Hall

Above Left Death watch beetles are one of our biggest problems

Above right Work was undertaken on the lime ash floor in the Gallery Chamber in 2002

A timeline of repair

Based on a variety of sources, including tree-ring dating, fabric evidence, studying styles and illustrations, we have been able to put together a rough timeline of how the house developed, and, later, was repaired.

Building

*c.*1503–8 Hall and east wing built

*c.*1508 East wing extended

*c.*1508–40 Chapel chancel added

*c.*1546 Porch and north-west wing built

*c.*1560–62 South range built

Between *c.*1560 and *c.*1600 Long Gallery and top of Gatehouse added

After 1582 Brewhouse range added

1559 Bay windows built

Before 1598 Chapel wall paintings produced

Probably post-1559 Probable insertion of chimney in Great Hall, Parlours and possibly elsewhere (the Great Hall's stack may be 17th-century)

Repairs

1655/6–1660 General works of pointing, repairing lead and glazing, mending and cleaning gutters, repairing roofs and chimney

1658 Philip Moreton measures up for repair work; crossbeams running between the roof trusses are put in

1659 Repairs to Gallery roof

*c.*1660 Huge consoles are installed in the Great Chamber to help support the Long Gallery

1662 Gallery roof painted and mended

1794–1815 Ongoing repairs to roofs, windows, brickwork, plaster, slates and casements

1797 Roof repairs undertaken after large parlour chimney blown down

By 1865 Large brick buttresses on east wall added, to help support the range containing the Long Gallery

1890s Elizabeth Moreton adds iron uprights and tie beams and undertakes extensive further restoration work around the building

1927–1935 Bishop Abraham continues the restoration programme started by Elizabeth, including significant works to timber and panelling

1951–2 Repairs to Great Hall and Parlour chimney and flues, and floor, oak plinth and panelling in the Little Parlour

1957 Programme of repairs including removal of the Great Hall's panelling, and identification and treatment of serious decay and beetle attack to timberwork

1966 Repairs carried out in Great Parlour and to Little Parlour chamber windows and panelling

1977 The National Trust begins a six-phase programme of structural repair

1990/1 A cantilevered steel frame support is inserted in the Long Gallery and the majority of the south range is repaired and many windows are replaced

Top to bottom Laying lime ash floor (first and second); repairs to the south range stairs; scaffolding on the front of the Little Tea Room during general repairs